SPORTS CARS COLORING BOOK

FAST FORWARD WITH DREAM CARS & ADVANCED MODELS

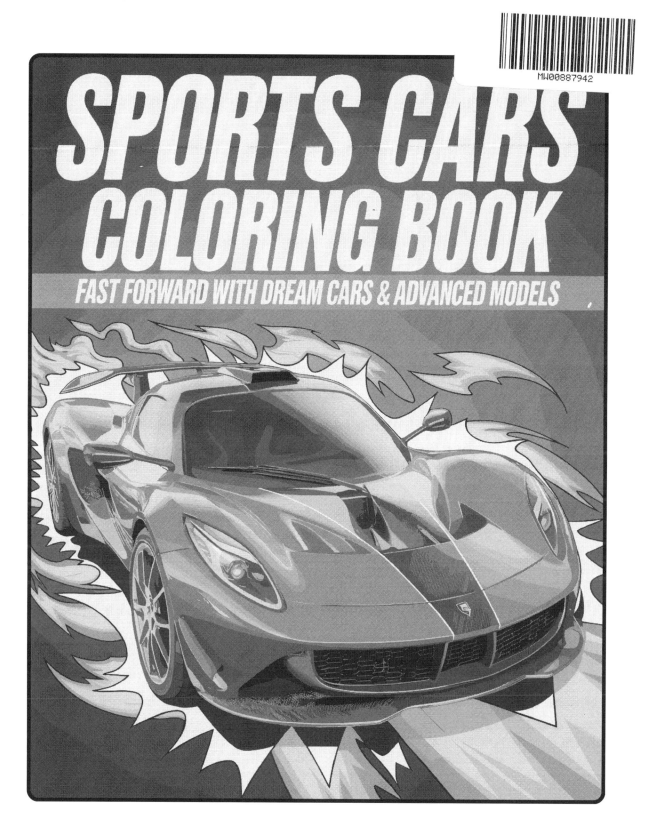

FANTASTIC CASTLING

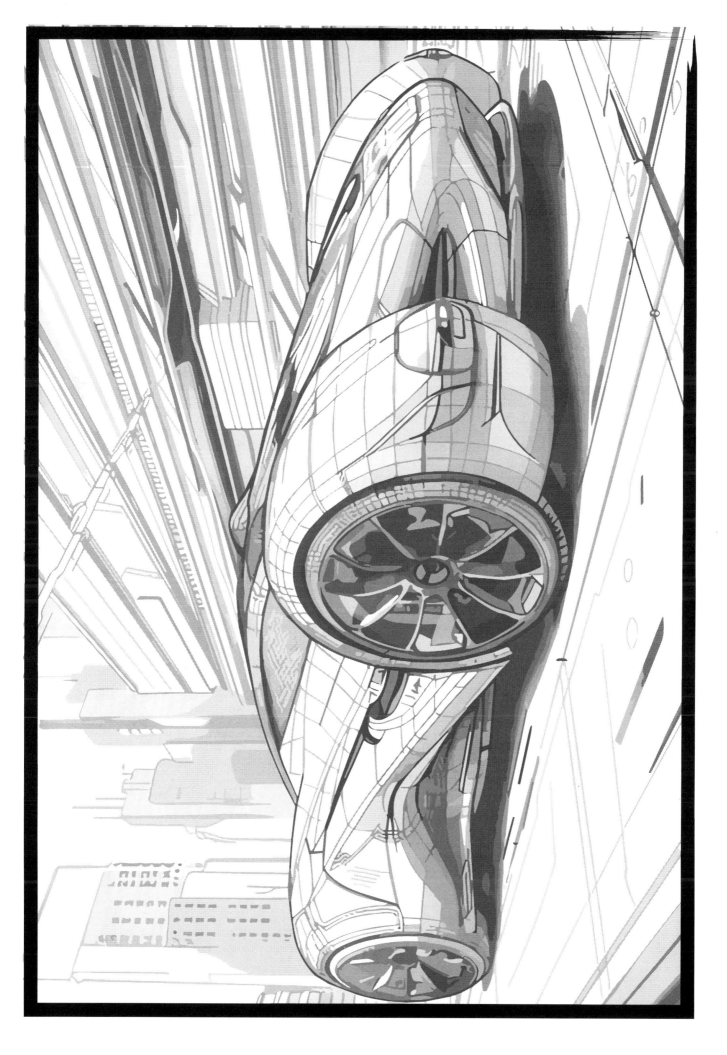

This page has been left blank on purpose.

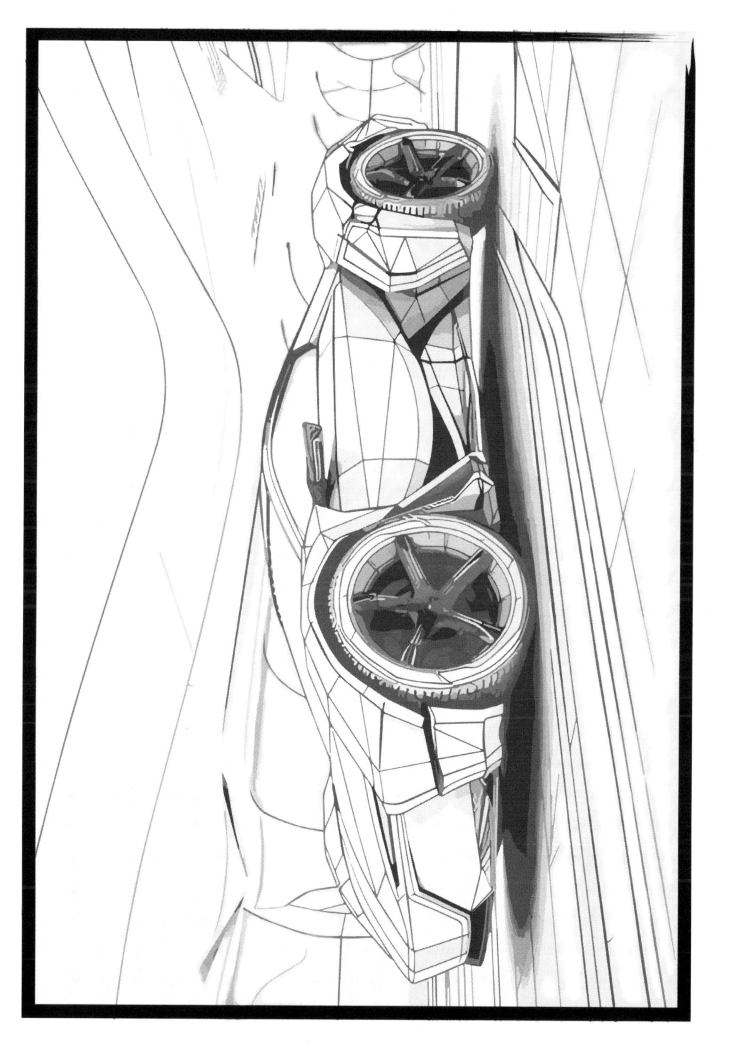

This page has been left blank on purpose.

This page has been left blank on purpose.

This page has been left blank on purpose.

This page has been left blank on purpose.

This page has been left blank on purpose.

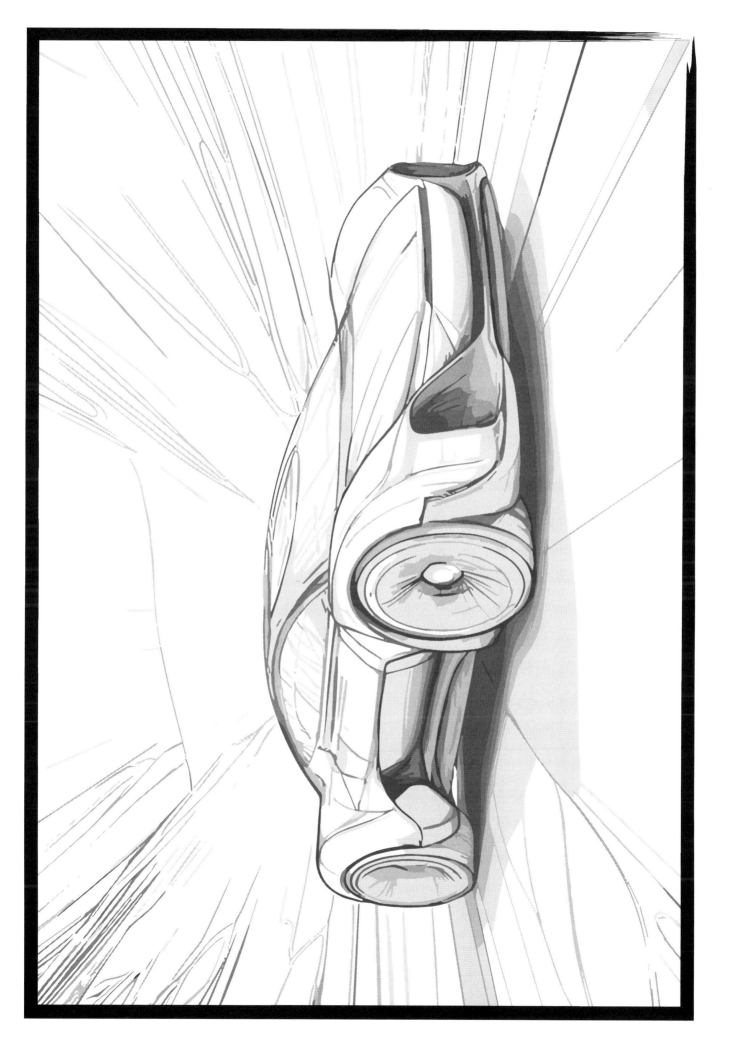

This page has been left blank on purpose.

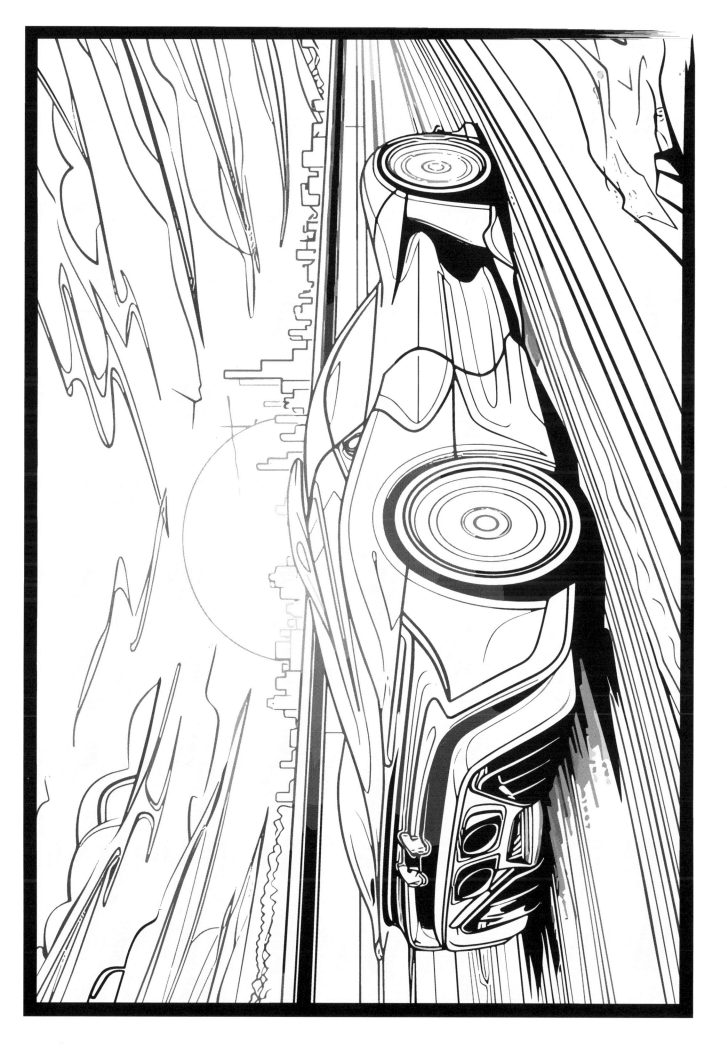

This page has been left blank on purpose.

This page has been left blank on purpose.

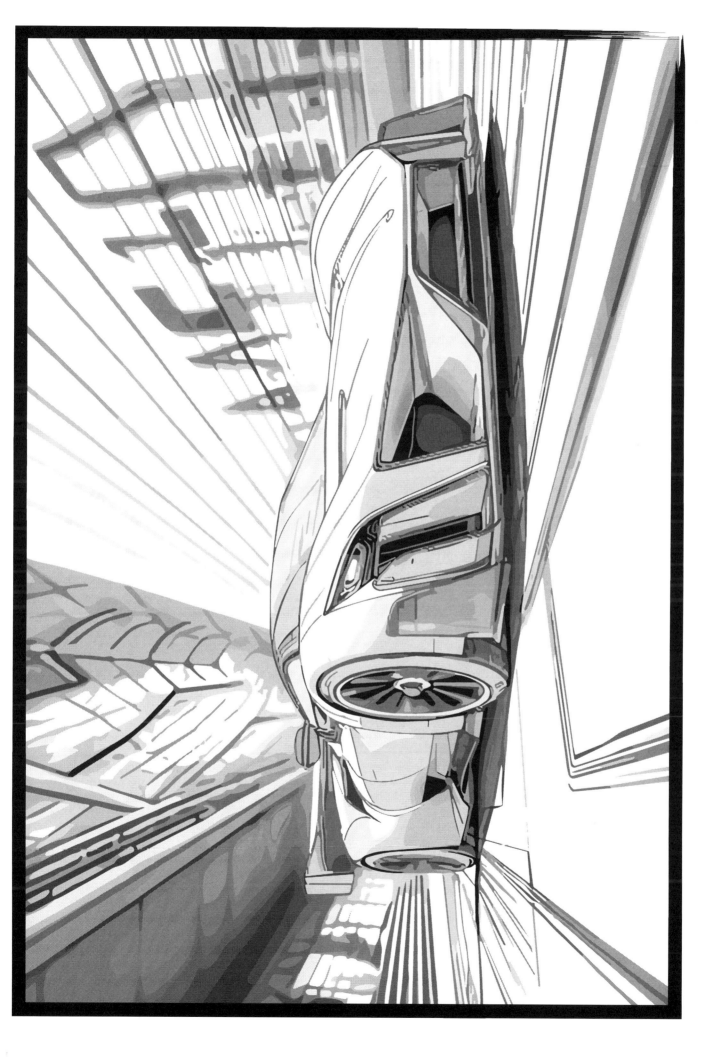

This page has been left blank on purpose.

This page has been left blank on purpose.

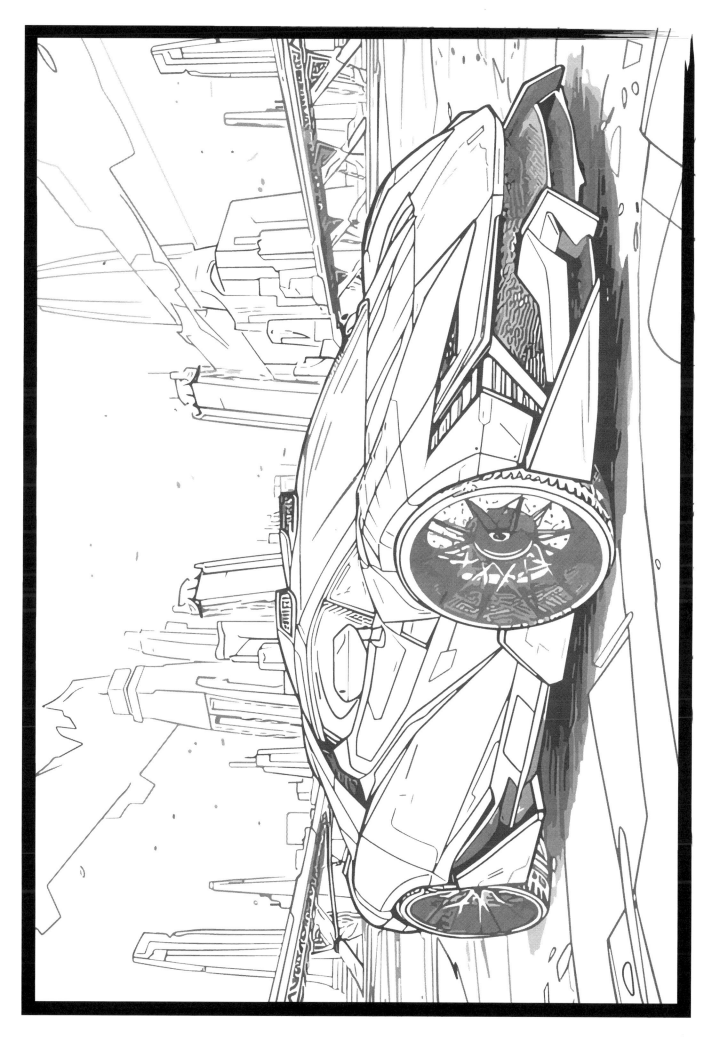

This page has been left blank on purpose.

This page has been left blank on purpose.

This page has been left blank on purpose.

This page has been left blank on purpose.

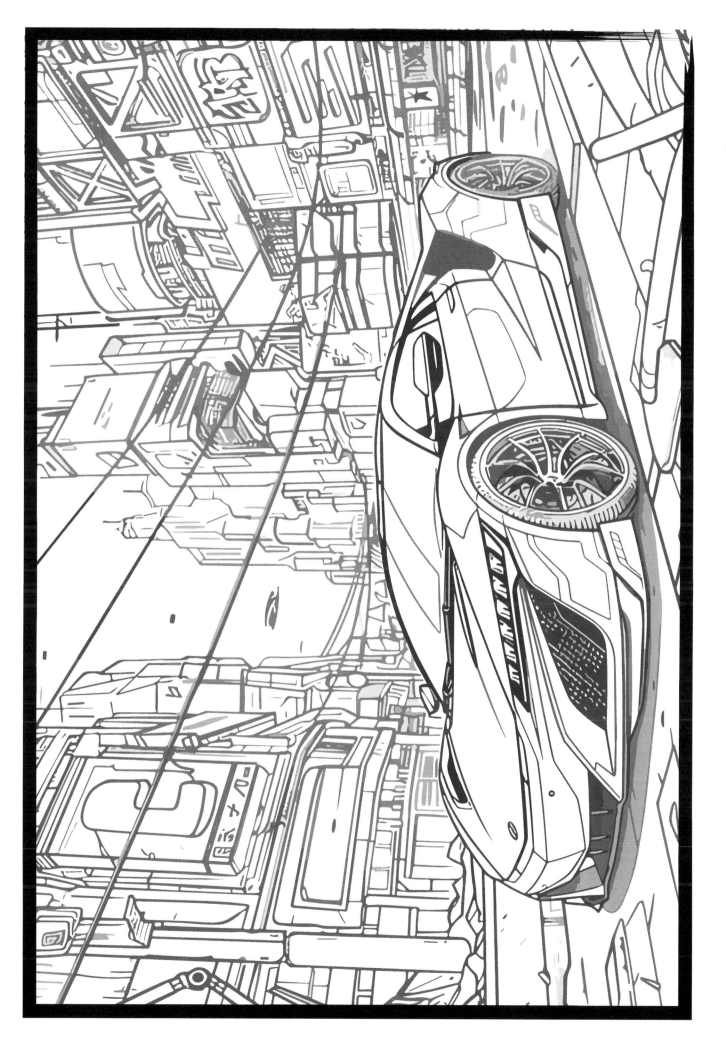

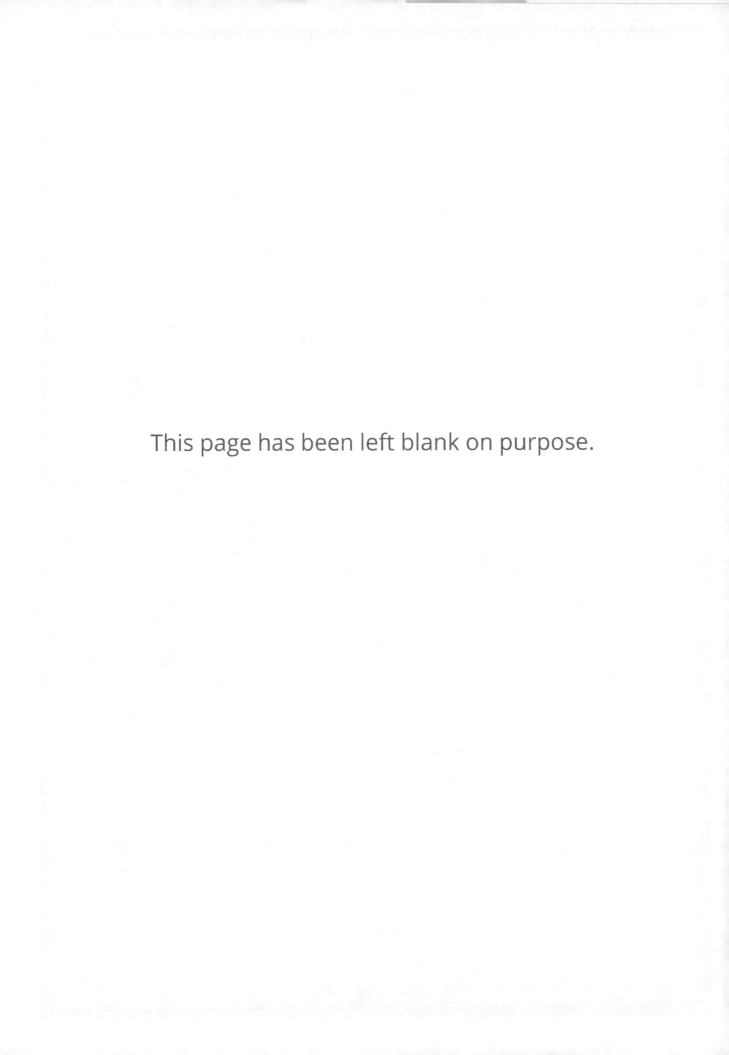

This page has been left blank on purpose.

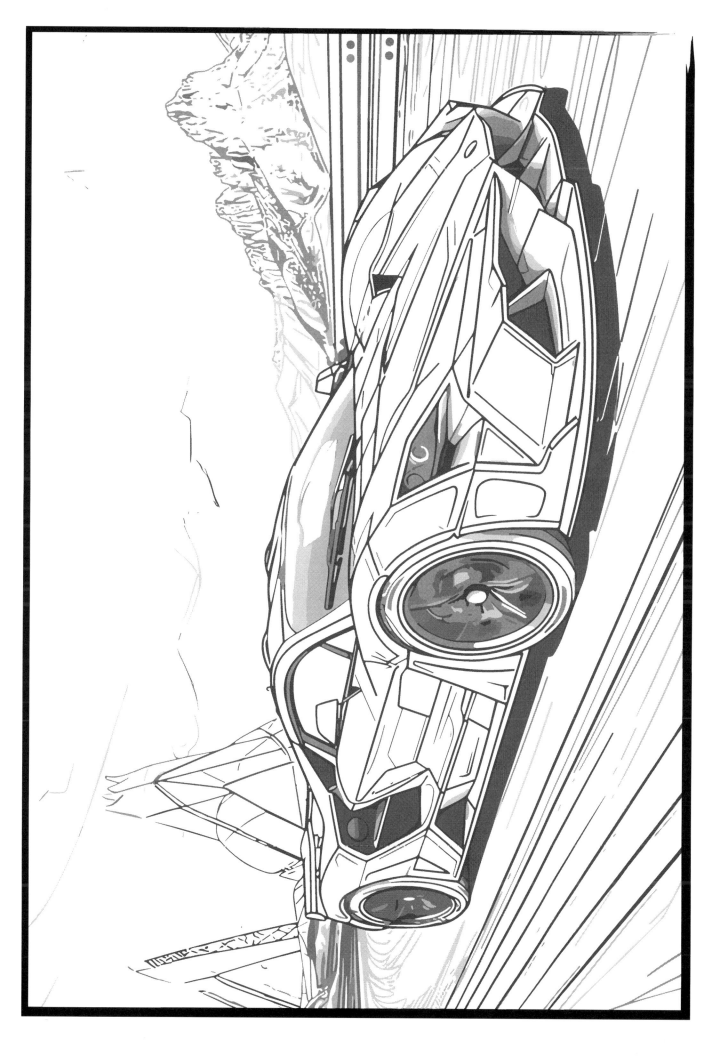

This page has been left blank on purpose.

This page has been left blank on purpose.

This page has been left blank on purpose.

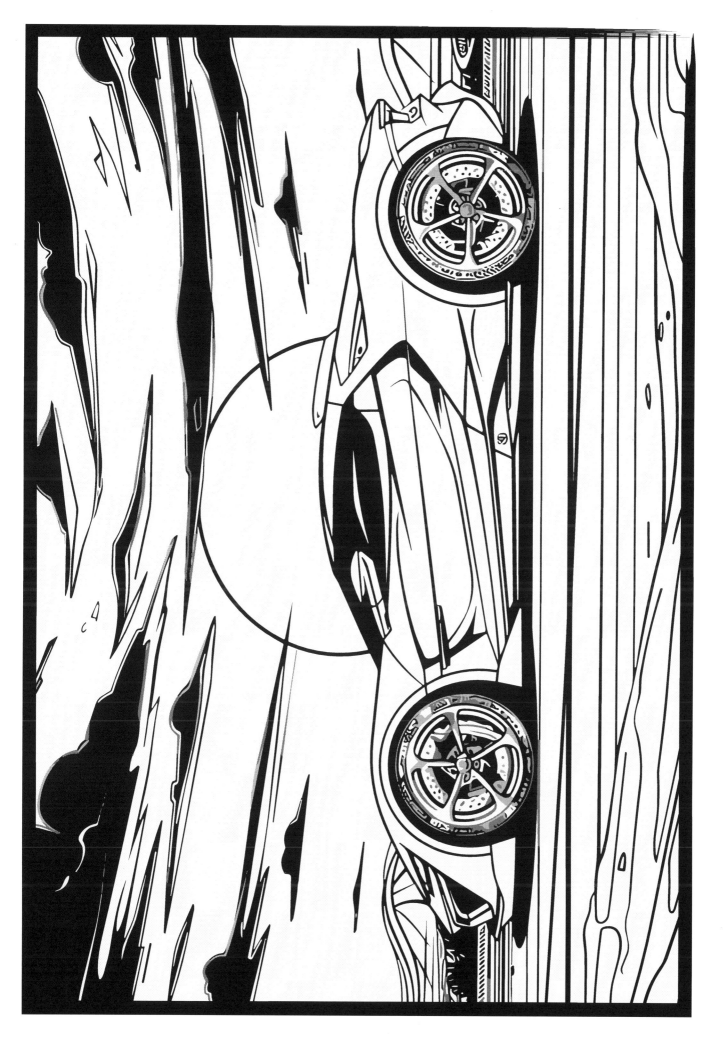

This page has been left blank on purpose.

This page has been left blank on purpose.

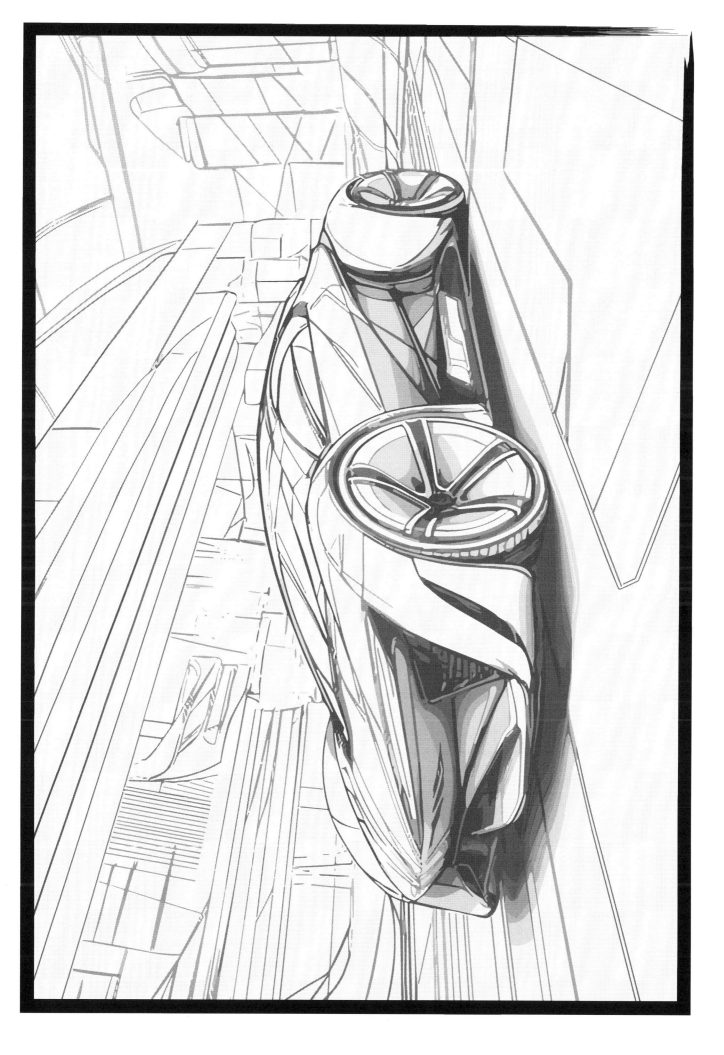

This page has been left blank on purpose.

This page has been left blank on purpose.

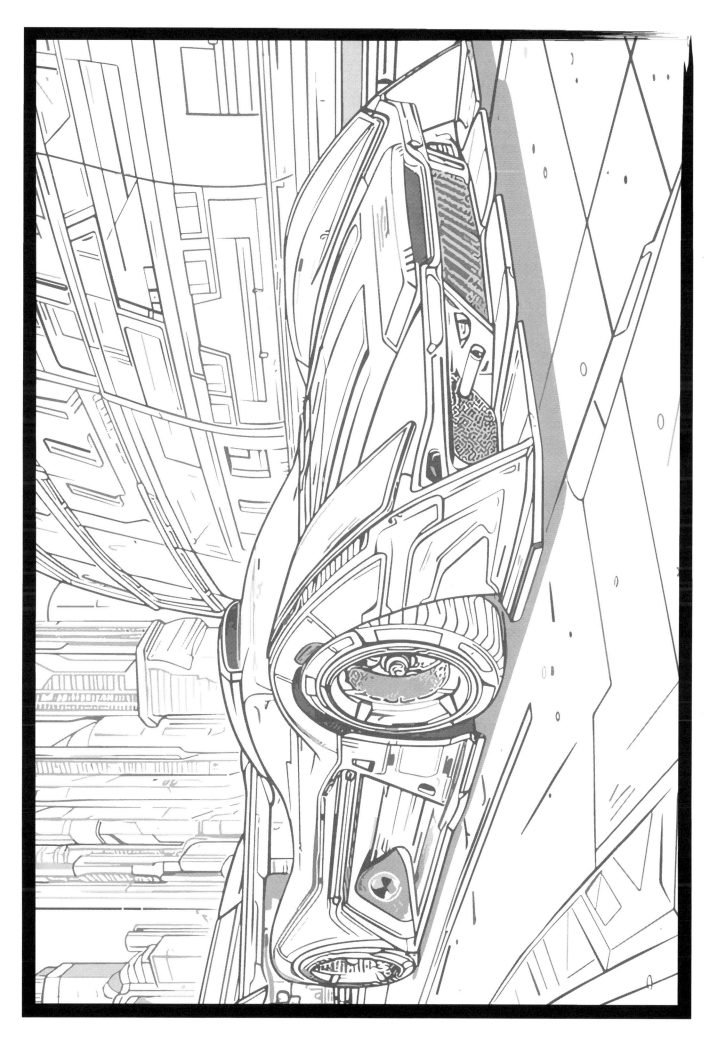

This page has been left blank on purpose.

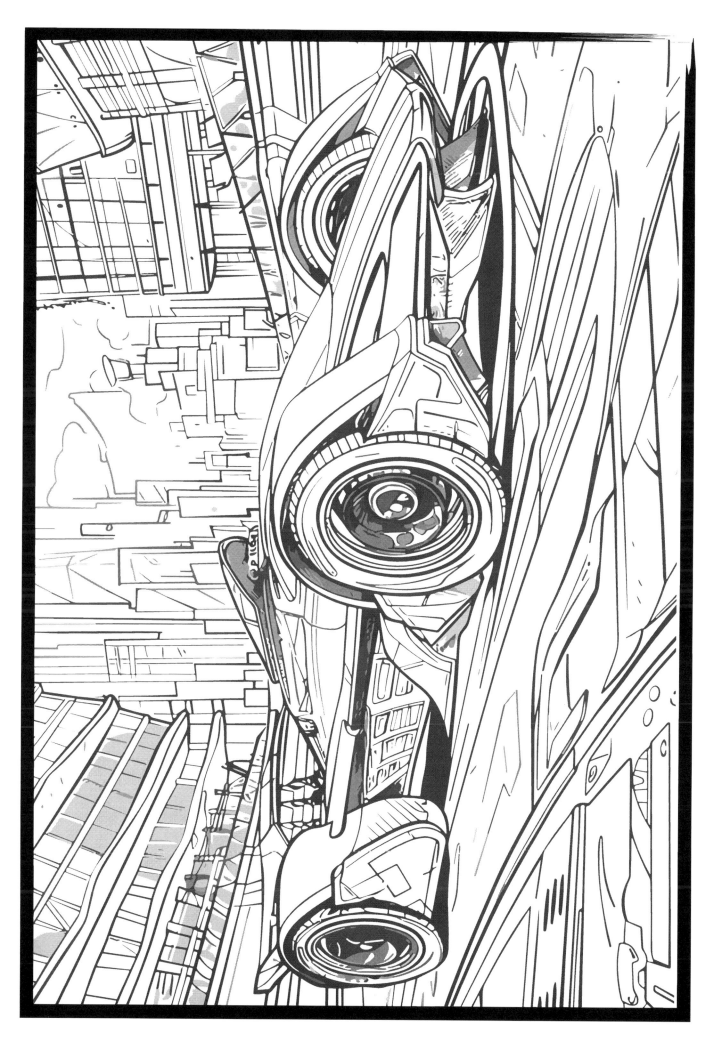

This page has been left blank on purpose.

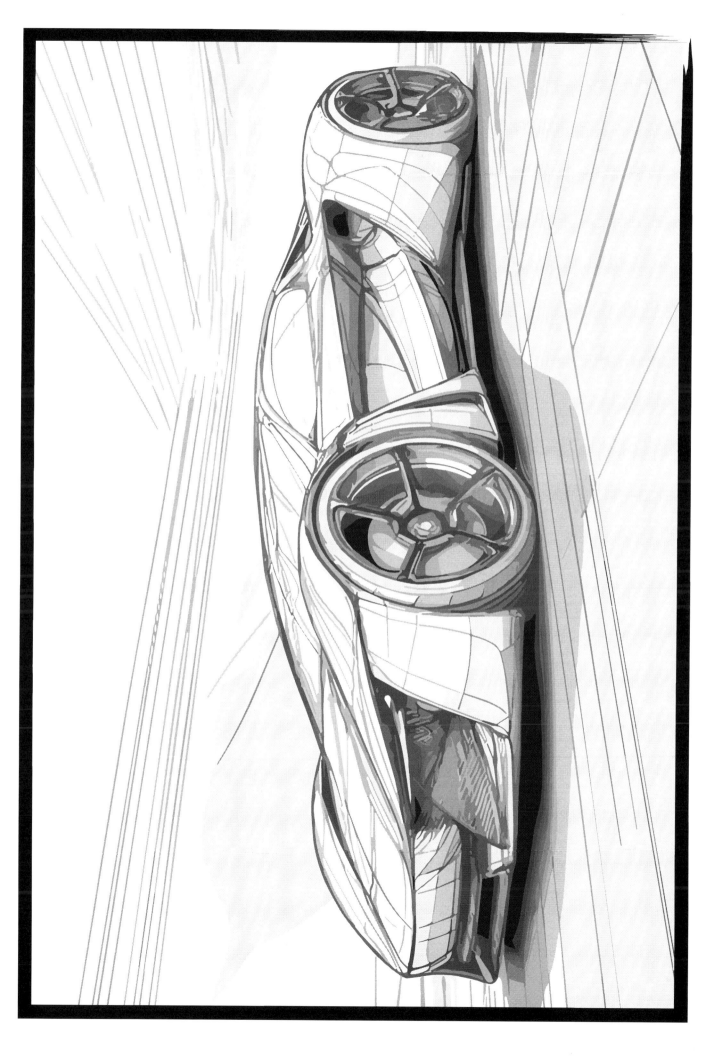

This page has been left blank on purpose.

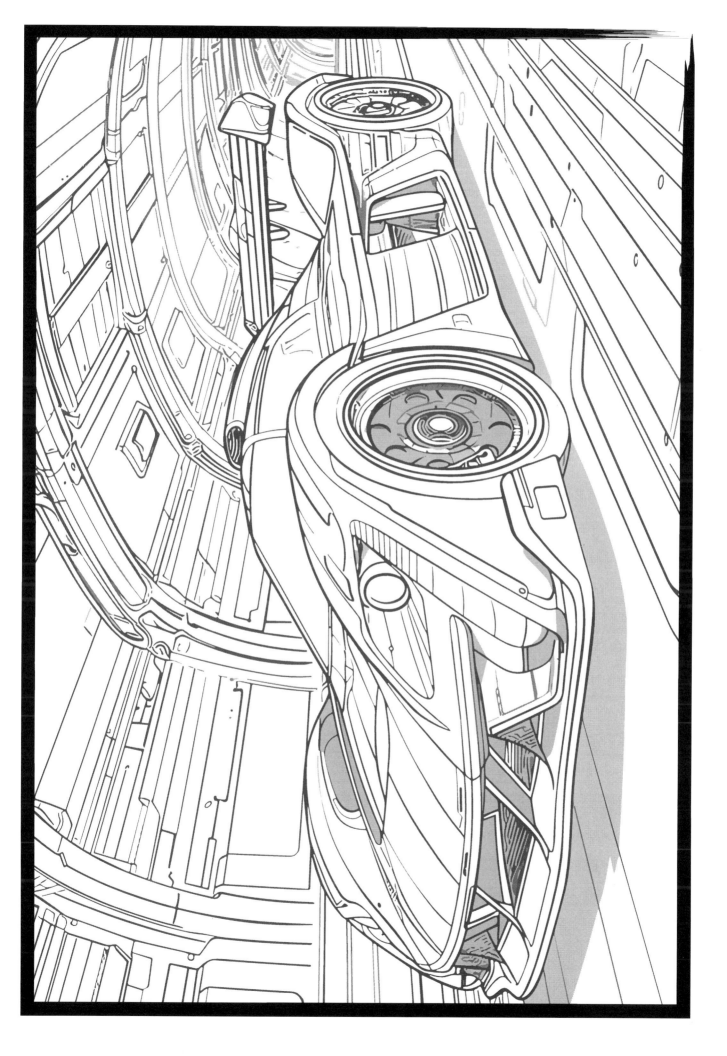

This page has been left blank on purpose.

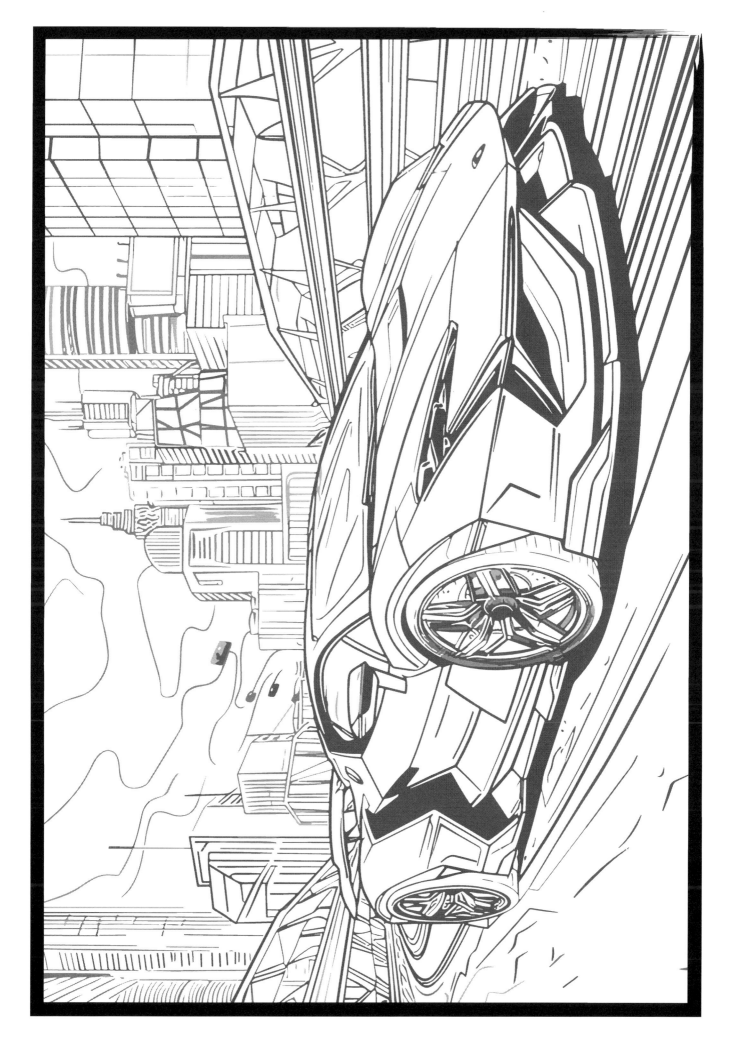

This page has been left blank on purpose.

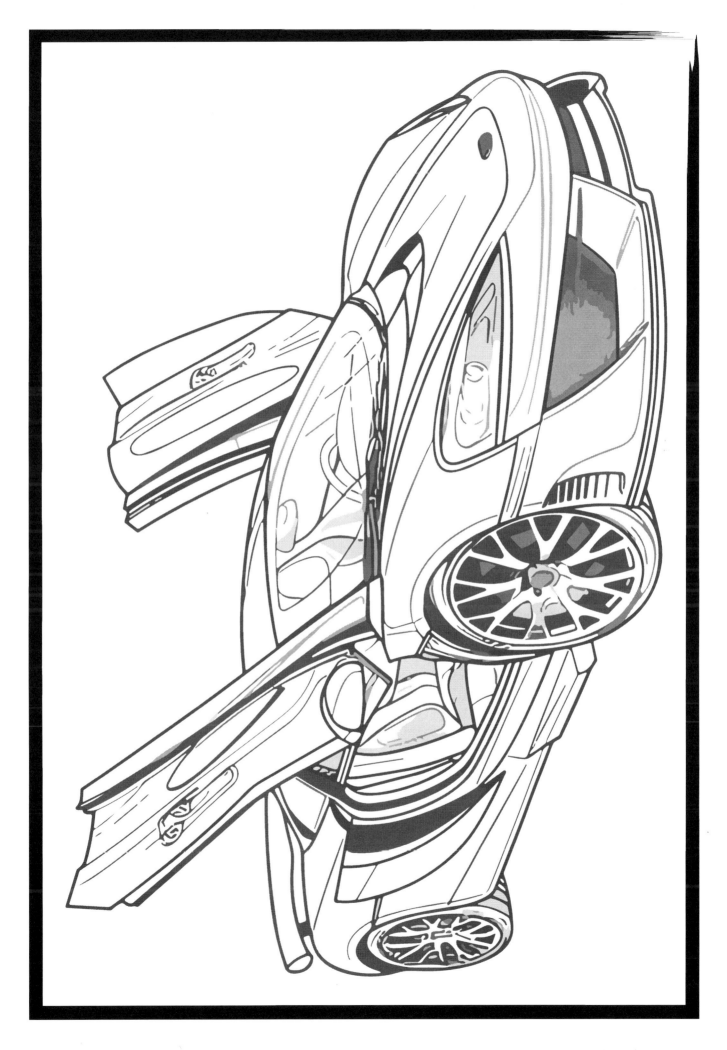

This page has been left blank on purpose.

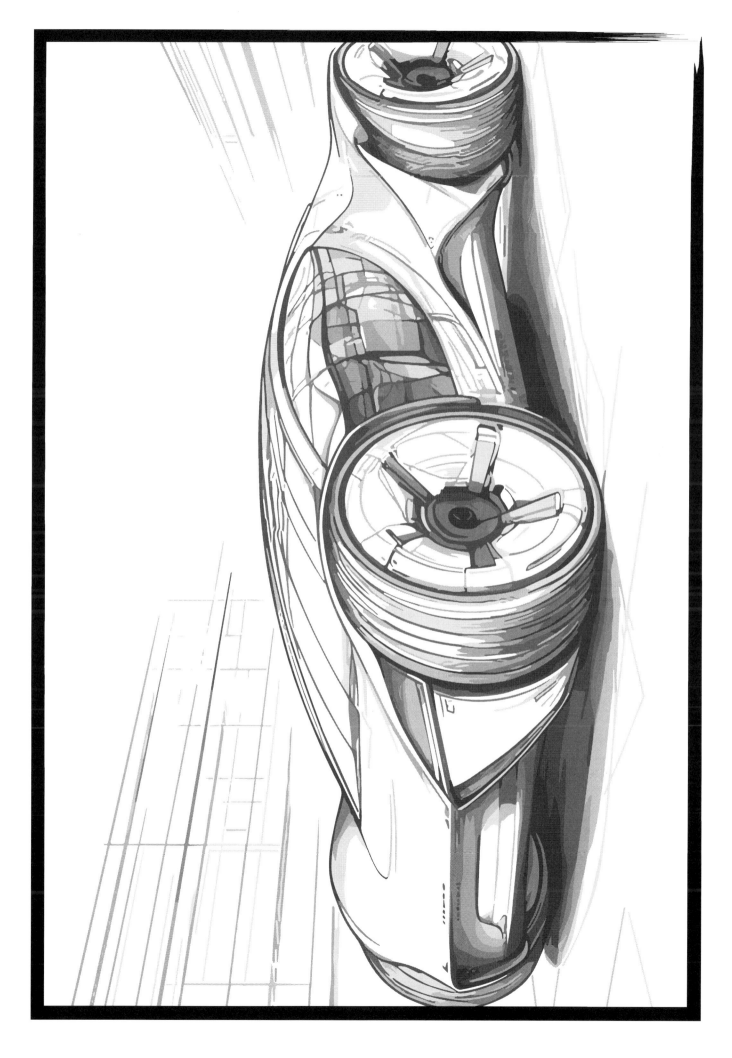

This page has been left blank on purpose.

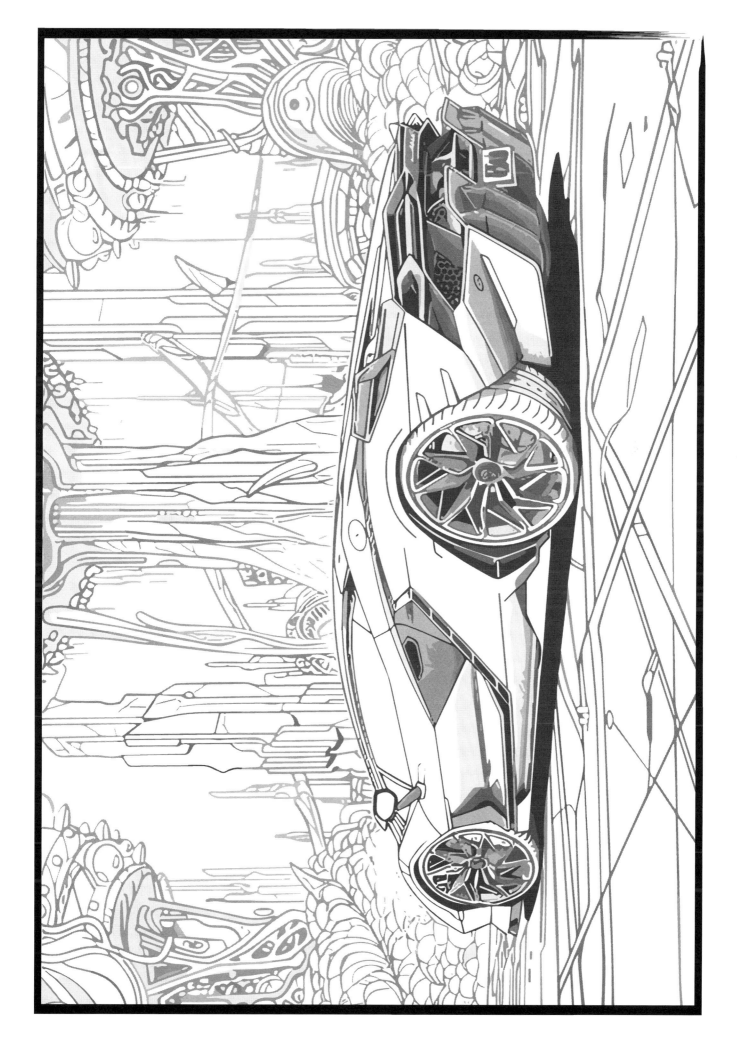

This page has been left blank on purpose.

This page has been left blank on purpose.

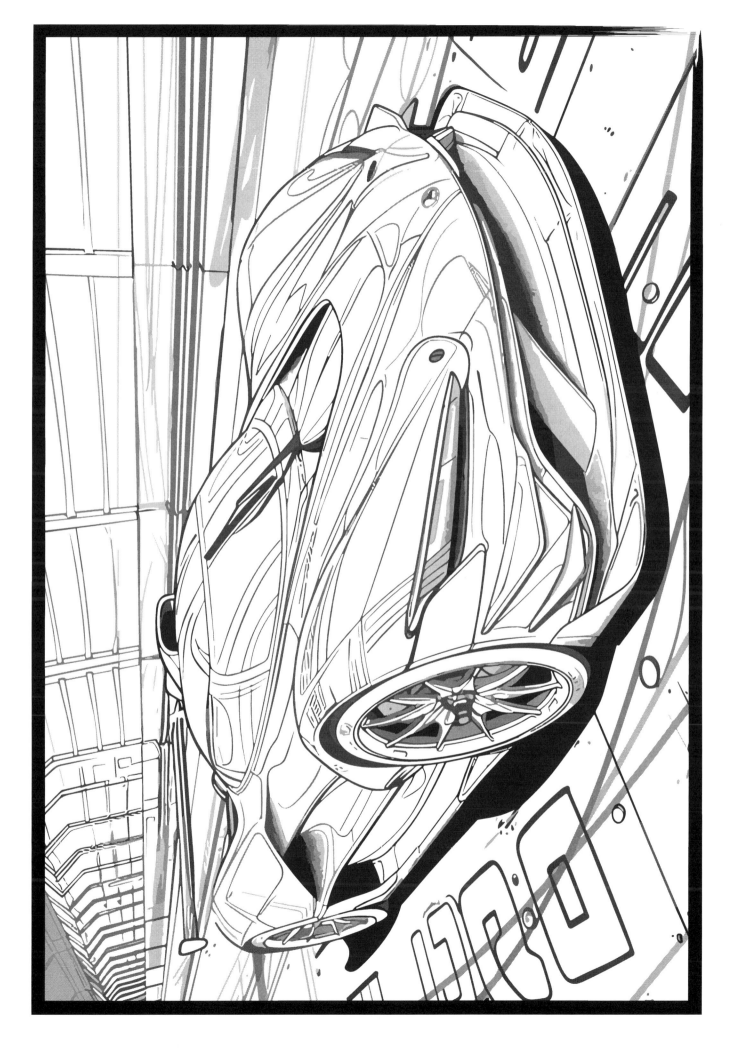

This page has been left blank on purpose.

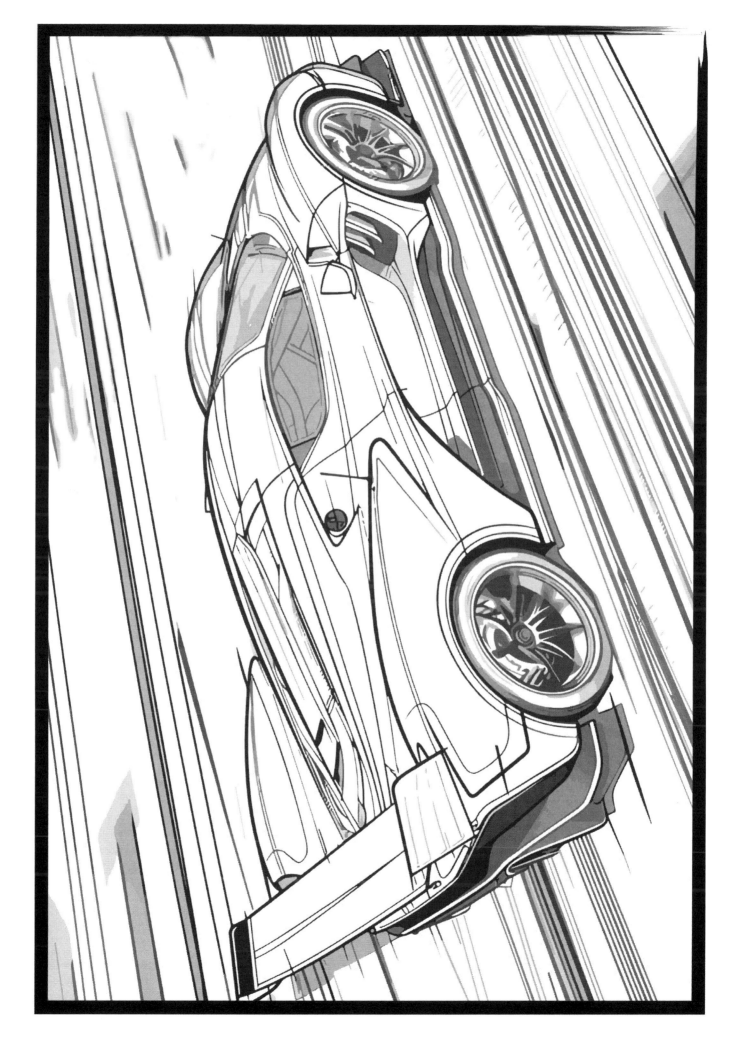

This page has been left blank on purpose.

This page has been left blank on purpose.

This page has been left blank on purpose.

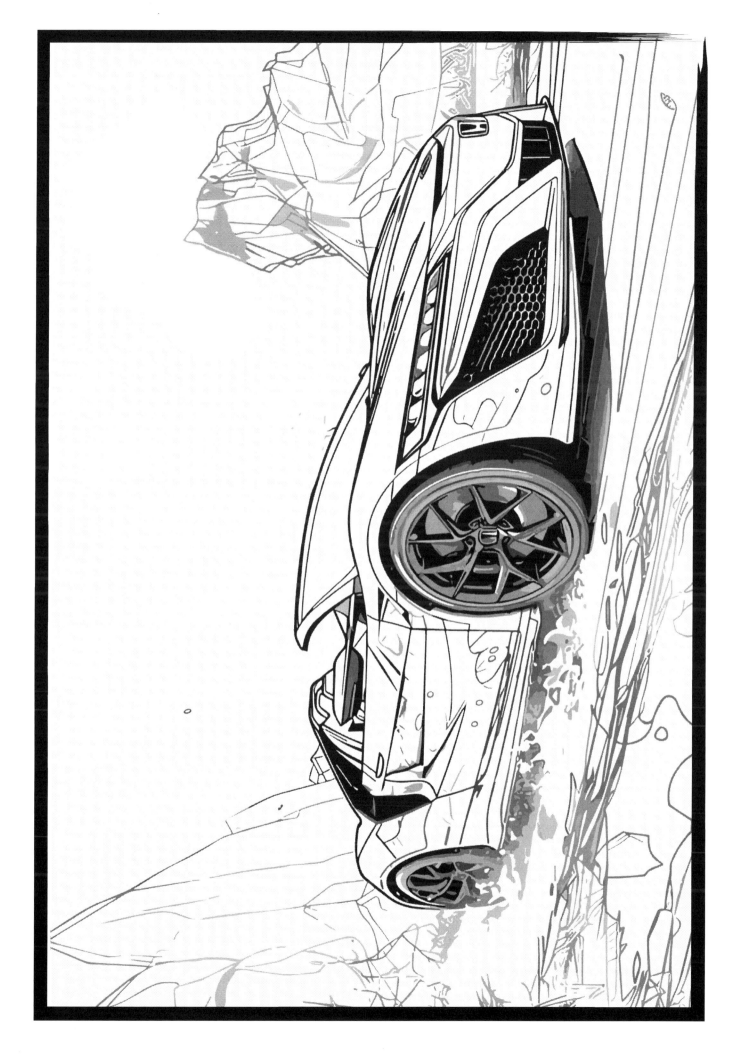

This page has been left blank on purpose.

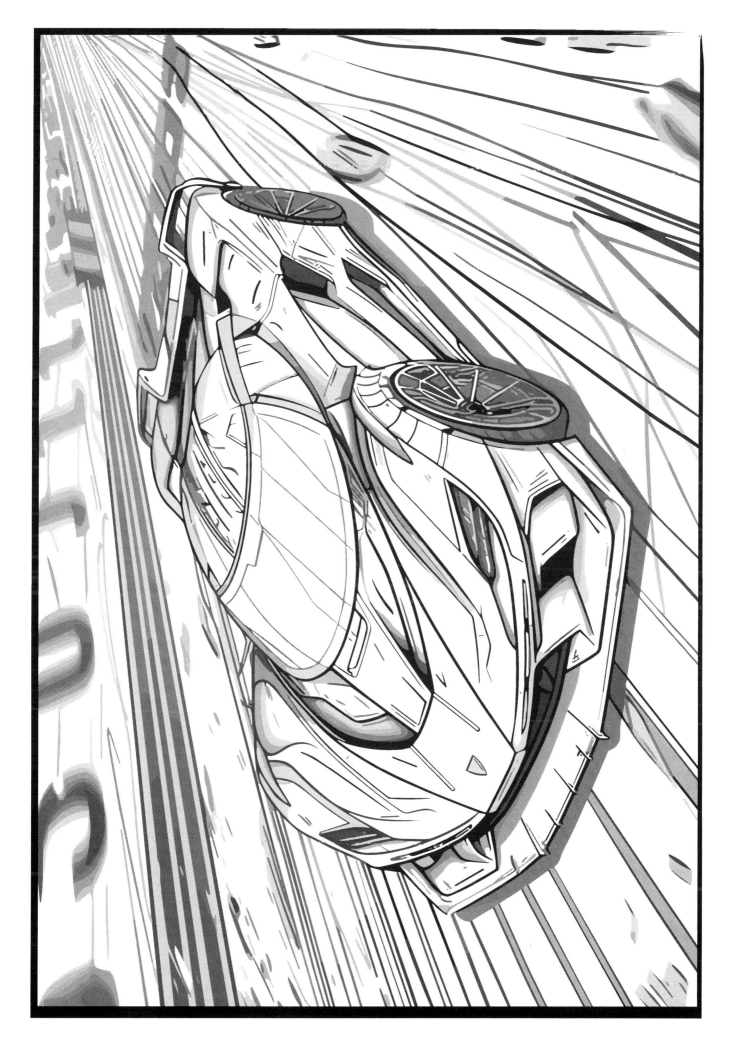

This page has been left blank on purpose.

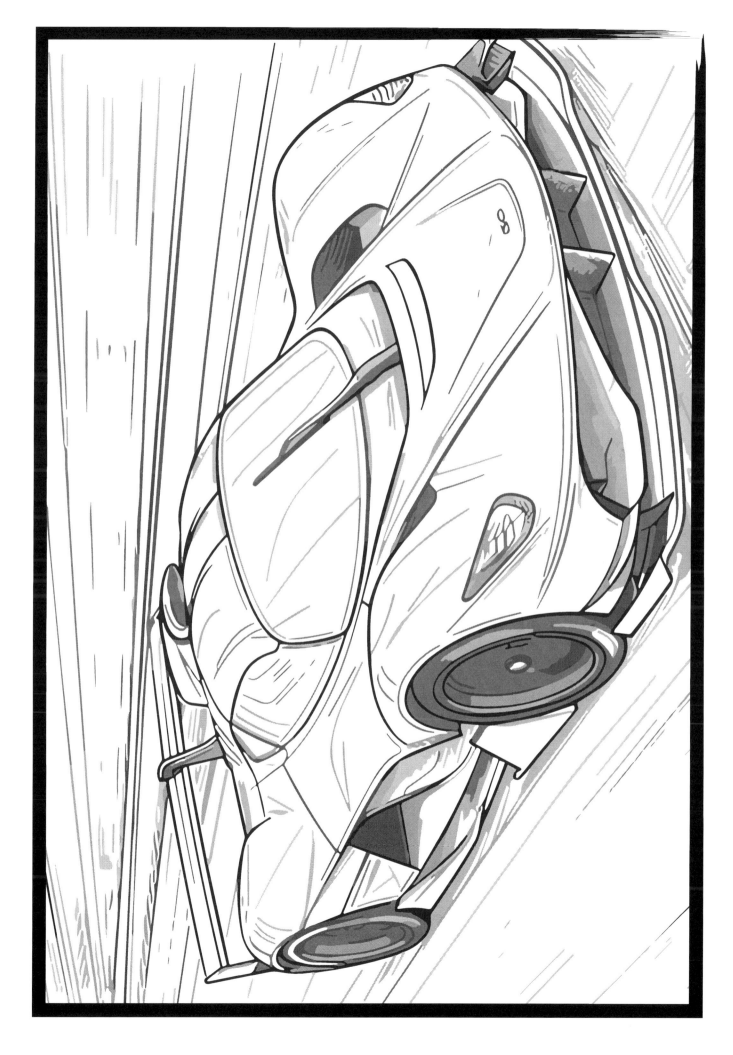

This page has been left blank on purpose.

This page has been left blank on purpose.

This page has been left blank on purpose.

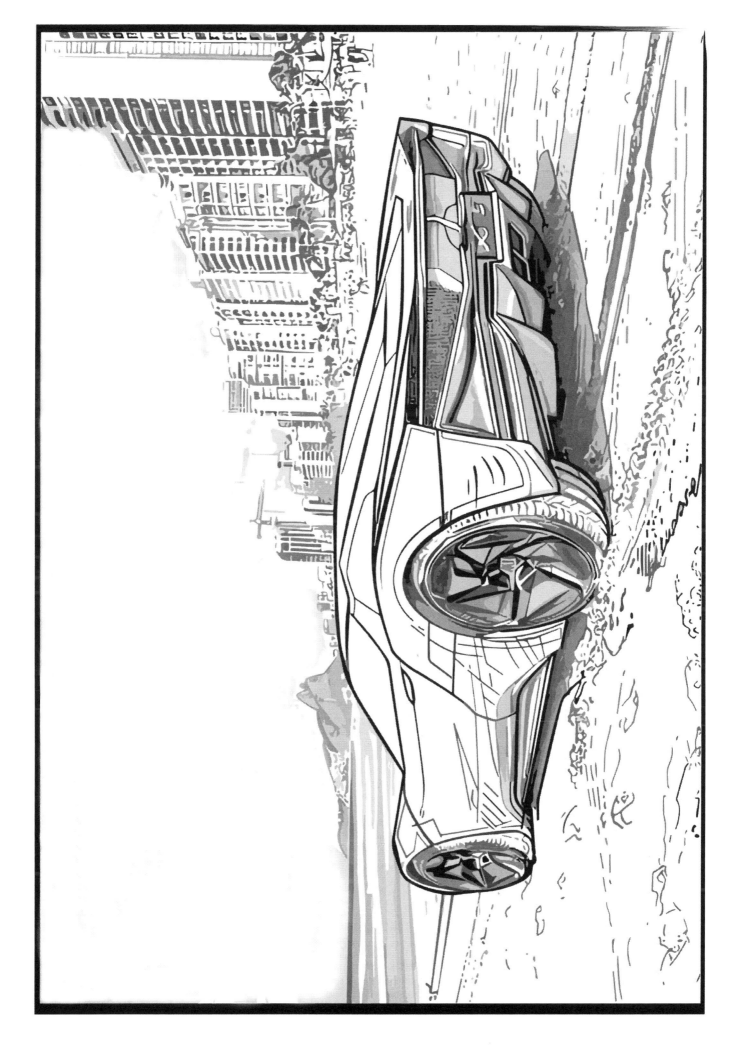

This page has been left blank on purpose.

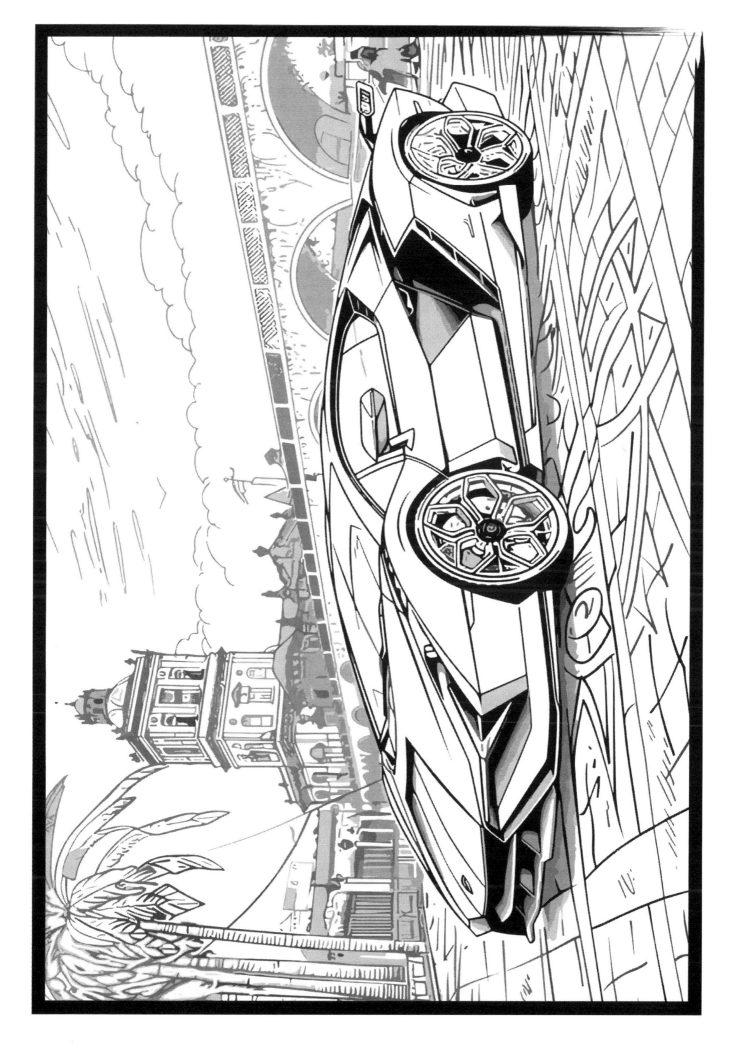

This page has been left blank on purpose.

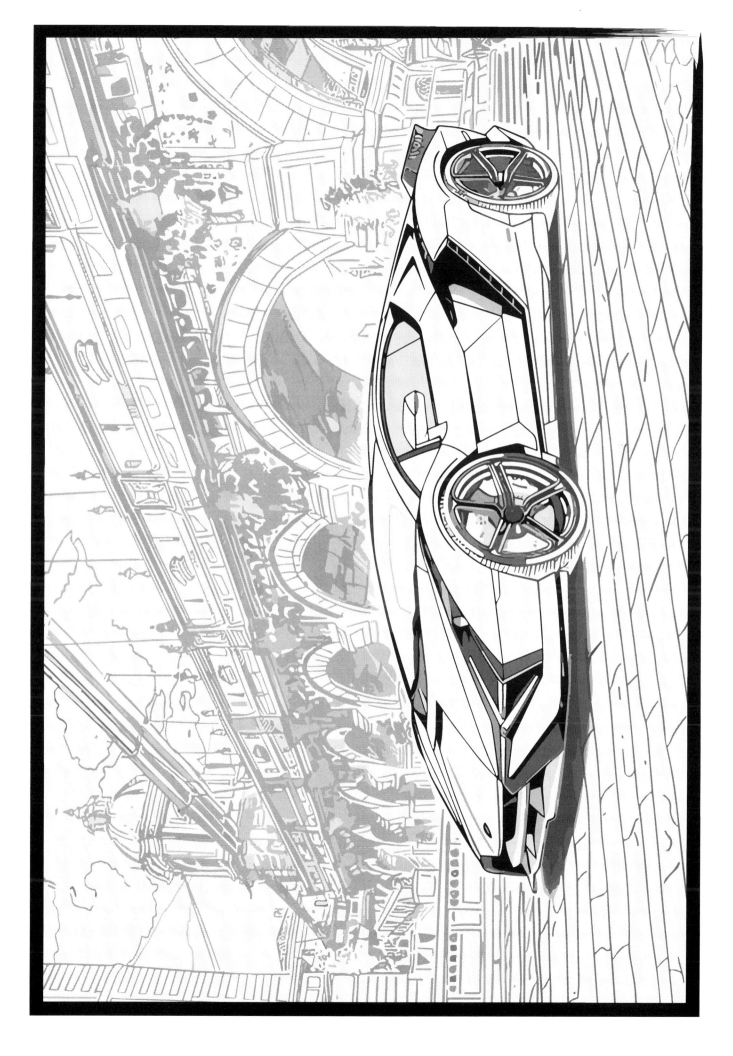

This page has been left blank on purpose.

This page has been left blank on purpose.

This page has been left blank on purpose.

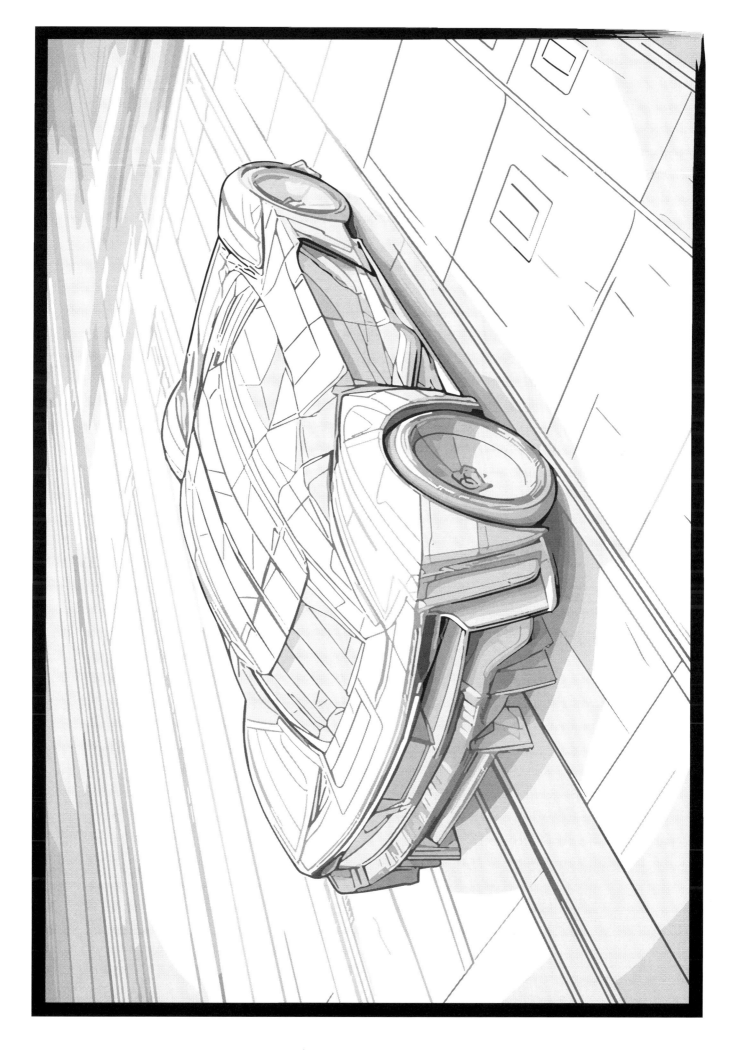

This page has been left blank on purpose.

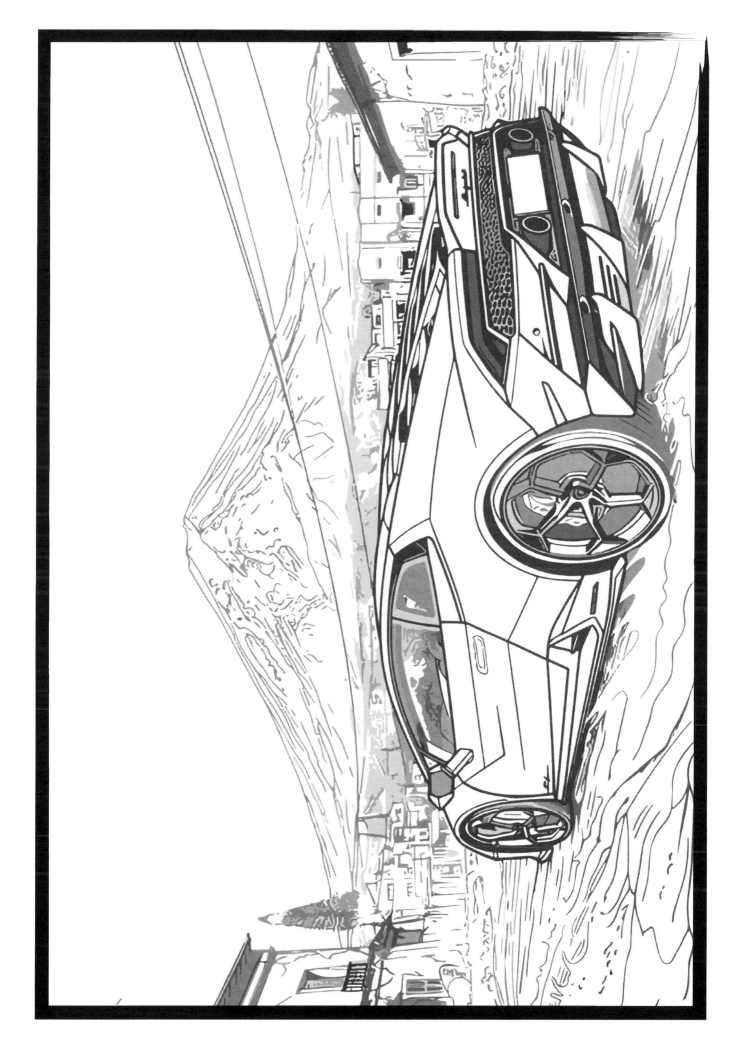

This page has been left blank on purpose.

This page has been left blank on purpose.

This page has been left blank on purpose.

This page has been left blank on purpose.

This page has been left blank on purpose.

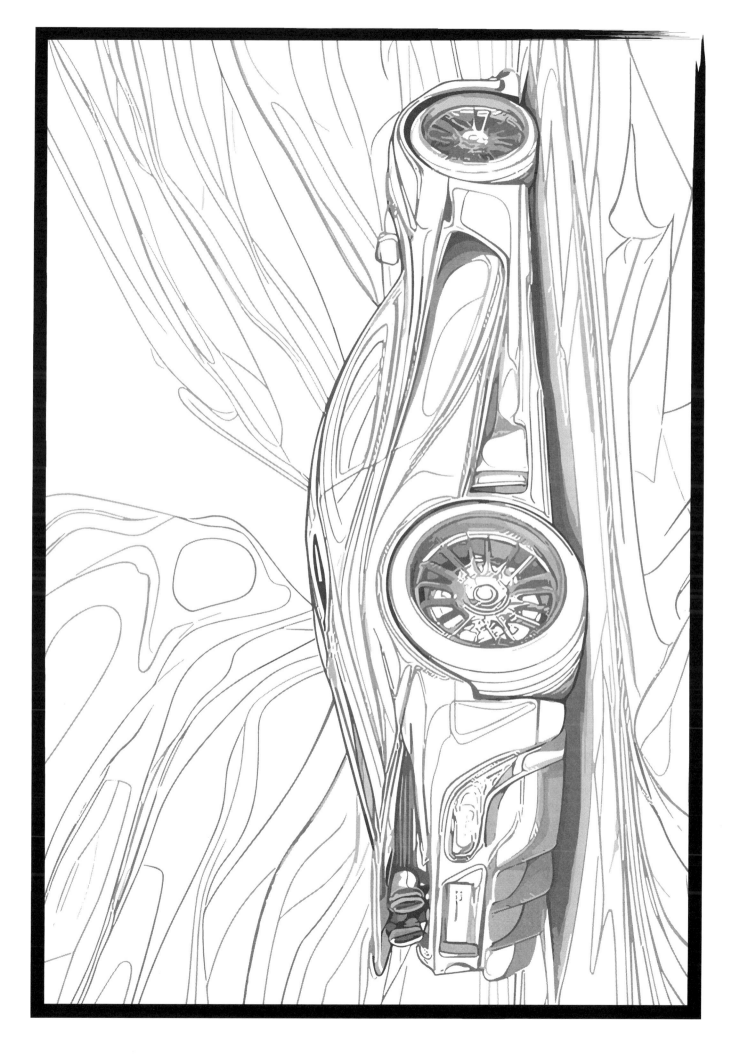

This page has been left blank on purpose.

Made in the USA
Monee, IL
29 November 2024

71561977R00061